HOW TO PURCHASE AND DEVELOP

COMMERCIAL REAL ESTATE

A Step by Step Guide for Success

ROBERT A. WEHRMEYER

Copyright © 2014 by Wehr Ventures, dba for Otali Solutions LLC

All Rights Reserved
Printed in the United States of America
Published by Wehr Publishing, dba for Otali Solutions LLC
San Antonio, Texas 78015
ISBN: 098453461X
ISBN 13: 978-0-9845346-1-6

To order additional copies of this book, please visit www.wehrventures.com.

WehrVentures
dba for Otali Solutions, LLC

ABOUT THE AUTHOR

Mr. Wehrmeyer is a Texas lawyer, commercial real estate developer, and part-time professor at the University of Texas-San Antonio, teaching real estate development and finance. In 2010, Bob published the book *The Complete Guide to Developing Commercial Real Estate, the Who, What, Where, Why and How Principles to Developing Commercial Real Estate* (updated and reprinted 2013). Now living in San Antonio, Bob and his wife of more than twenty five-years, Cindy, have two children, daughter Ashley and son Trey.

ACKNOWLEDGMENTS

Thanks, appreciation, and admiration to the staff, faculty, and students of University of Texas in San Antonio for giving me the opportunity to be a part of their lives and their great institution. Love to my wife, Cindy, daughter, Ashley, and son, Trey, for their patience and understanding of my somewhat quirky nature.

CONTENTS

SECTION 2:

Can the Project make Money? 10 Simple Steps

INTRODUCTION

Introduction

Lease Revenue Analysis

Estimating *Project Revenue* — Simple Analysis

Introduction

Cap Rate Valuation

Project Value = Net Operating Income/Cap Rate

Estimating Project Value

Introduction

Three Major Construction Costs

Land Cost

Construction and Design Cost

Tenant Improvement and Lease Commission

Estimating Project Construction Cost

Steps Five, Six, Seven, and Eight

Introduction

Construction Loan — Debt Service Coverage Ratio

Construction Loan — Interest Only

Construction Loan — Loan to Cost and Loan to Value Limitations

Estimating Cost Of The Construction Loan

Introduction

The Equity Investor

Introduction

Project Profit

Distribution of Profit

SECTION 3:
How To Purchase And Rehab An Existing Commercial Building

INTRODUCTION

Purchasing the Project or Building

Major Rehabilitation and Repair Cost

Making the Lease Space Suitable for Tenants and Users

Tenant Improvement Costs

Real Estate Brokerage Commission Costs

The Cost of Borrowing the Money

Can the Project Make Money?

PART 1:
HOW TO PURCHASE AND DEVELOP COMMERCIAL REAL ESTATE

A STEP-BY-STEP GUIDE FOR SUCCESS

INTRODUCTION

A few years ago I wrote the book *The Complete Guide to Developing Commercial Real Estate, the Who, What, Where, Why and How Principles to Developing Commercial Real Estate*. The book was intended to create a useful guide for the reader to understand the basic steps involved in converting a vision into a commercial real estate development project. The book was a result of my experience as a developer and focused on an important central theme. The central theme set forth in the book is financing. The importance of financing or money in getting a project built. From the developer's perspective, the well-known golden rule of real estate—location, location, location—might well be translated to finance, finance, finance. If a developer can finance a project, he can get it built.

The Complete Guide to Developing Commercial Real Estate, the Who, What, Where, Why and How Principles to Developing Commercial Real Estate is based on the theory that meeting the needs and demands of potential financing partners should force the developer to ask and answer all the critical questions to move a new or rehab development project forward. Getting someone to finance a project with both debt and equity addresses most if not all of the critical questions that a developer should be able to ask and answer to put a commercial real estate project on the right path for success. In this book, part one of a series, we begin to explore specific issues related to the "how" principle in the who, what, where, why, and how book; specifically how to find tenants, attract financing, and successfully purchase the location and build or purchase a commercial real estate project.

What is commercial real estate development?

What is success in commercial real estate development? What does it mean to be a successful commercial real estate developer? Commercial real estate development is the ability to take a piece of land or existing building(s) and create something of value, something that will attract tenants, users, and ultimately buyers. It's that simple. You want to build something that a person, business, or municipality will pay you rent to use, people will want to live in, use, or visit, and a buyer will want to purchase. Of course, you typically want to build or rehab something that will result in a profit and you can be proud of. So how do you get started?

If you are reading this book, you most likely have an idea, vision, location, existing building, or a tenant expressing a need for space. So how do you take the first steps to assess the land/building, potential tenants, financing partners, and even future buyers? Once a developer formulates an idea, there is typically one key question that follows: can the project make money? This one question is often difficult for many nonfinancially oriented developers to answer. This books attempts to help the reader ask and answer the question by first reviewing the basic fundamentals of commercial real estate development (section one), outlining the key assumptions and a simple step-by-step process to determine if the project can make money (section two), and then explores the true cost of purchasing and rehabbing an existing commercial building (section three).

Look for this arrow ◄ throughout this book; it will indicate important issues or concepts.

.

PREFACE

Commercial real estate development can be risky business. Ask anyone who was involved in commercial real estate in the early eighties or when the most recent recession hit in 2009. Most real estate professionals will tell you that when real estate is good it is very good and when real estate is bad it is extremely bad. In fact, the commercial real estate economic "down cycle" historically lasts a lot longer than the "up cycle." To make things more difficult, the real estate developer sits at the top of the real estate iceberg. When there is market meltdown, such as what occurred in 2009, the developer can do little but tread water.

That being said, there is great satisfaction and achievement in weathering the multitude of risks and issues associated with bringing a new or redeveloped project to market. Not only is a successful development project personally fulfilling but the financial value that can be created is significant. The reason for this is fundamental to the development process—tenants. Tenants agree to pay you rent. Often tenants agree to pay you rent for long periods of time. They agree to pay you rent for long periods of time by entering into legal binding agreements called leases. That's pretty much it. Get high-quality tenants to sign long-term leases to pay you rent and you are well on your way to creating something of value.

However, it's not always easy to attract these valuable tenants; there is a lot of competition out there. The key to attracting these valuable tenants is often location, the golden rule of real estate—location, location, location. Of course, even if you sign up these key tenants you still need to buy the land or building, build or renovate and repair the project, get the tenants moved in, and manage or operate the facility—so much to do, so little time. This book and the books to follow will focus on specific key issues related to commercial real estate development and hopefully result in saving the reader not only time but a little money as well.

SECTION 1:
THREE KEYS TO DEVELOPING COMMERCIAL REAL ESTATE

In this section:

Location Attracts Tenants, Tenants Pay Rent,

Rent-Paying Tenants Attract Money

Chapter 1: The Money

INTRODUCTION

Developing commercial real estate can be complicated. However, as with many things in life, when you analyze the basic components you often find that the process is simpler than it appears. There is one fundamental component that stretches across each of the major areas of the development process—from buying the land, to building or renovating the building, to attracting tenants, to managing the space, and even refinancing or selling the real estate project. This single component is money. All development projects need *money*. One must acquire the land, pay for certain upfront costs, pay to get the project built or renovated, and pay to support the building while finding enough tenants to fill it.

A THE FINANCING

1 THE CONSTRUCTION LOAN

Since development projects can be expensive, most developers look to third parties such as *commercial banks* and *investors* to supply the money needed to *finance* the project. If developers can finance a project, they can get it built. Getting financing, therefore, becomes the single biggest obstacle to moving from the *developer's vision* to construction, completion, and, finally, an open, operating, and successful development project. Almost all commercial real estate construction projects are financed by a majority of *debt*. The debt is usually in the form of a *construction loan* from a commercial bank and will typically constitute somewhere between 60–80 percent of the project cost. The neat thing about construction loans is that you pay only *interest* during construction and for a short period thereafter and then must refinance or pay off the loan.

2 THE EQUITY

The remaining portion of the project cost, the portion not funded by the bank construction loan, is often referred to as *equity*. Equity can come from many sources: equity can come from the developer, the land the project is to be built on, or from third-party investors. Remember, the bank only lends a portion of the money needed to complete the project (60-80 percent). The equity investment is the first money invested and funds the difference. Together, the construction loan and the equity investment make up the money needed to cover the project cost and are often referred to as the development project *capital stack*.

Most developers realize early on in the process that closing the construction loan is the most important step in a new development project becoming a reality. With the closing of the construction loan, a project moves from the stage of hoping to be built to a high likelihood it will be built. Therefore, meeting the needs and demands of the construction lender and the equity investors becomes the single most important factor in moving a development project forward.

That being said, financing for a new development project is not always easy to obtain. It can take many months, if not years, to find and close acceptable project financing. Although obtaining construction financing and equity investment may sound complicated, once again there is a single fundamental component that attracts almost every construction lender and equity investor to a commercial *real estate development project*.

Chapter 2: The Most Valuable Asset in a Commercial Real Estate Project

INTRODUCTION

In chapter one, we pointed out how complicated developing commercial real estate can seem unless you focus on the most important aspects of each phase. We also pointed out in chapter one that there is a fundamental component that stretches across each of the major areas of the development process, from buying the land or building, to construction of the project or renovation, to attracting tenants, to managing the space as landlord, and even refinancing or selling the completed project. This single component is money. All development projects need money. Since development projects can be expensive, most developers look to third parties such as commercial banks and investors to supply the money needed to "finance" the development project.

So how do you get a commercial bank and equity investors to finance the project? Once again focusing on the single most important component supplies the answer. The single most important factor in attracting money (financing) to a development project is the belief that the investors will get paid back (and hopefully make a little money). The most reliable way to prove to investors that they will get paid back is to attract rent-paying tenants[1] to the project.

◼ THE *TENANT*

The tenant is the most valuable asset in any commercial real estate development project. Sign up the right tenant or *tenant mix* and you may be able to choose from a pool of eager construction lenders and equity investors to finance the development project. What makes the tenant so important? The tenant is the person or entity that will enter into a long-term agreement to pay *rent*, bring people to the site, and make it attractive for other tenants and businesses. Rent creates cash flow, and cash flow helps

---

[1] The word *tenant* is an old French term and roughly translates to "one who is holding," such as one who is holding occupancy of a farm or building..

lenders and investors form a reasonable belief that they will get paid back. Of course, in a development project, certain tenants are more valuable than others. Most lenders and investors want to see tenants with a long history of operational success, solid financials, well-established brand or niche, and a financially stable *parent company* or owner to *guarantee* the long-term commitment or binding lease agreement.

THE LEASE AGREEMENT

The *lease agreement* might be the most important document a developer can produce. It is the document that will be given the most weight by lenders and equity investors in determining their desire to lend or invest. The lease agreement establishes a legal obligation on the part of the tenant to pay the developer rent often over a long period of time. Of course, getting a tenant to sign a long-term lease is not that simple. Remember, the building(s) may not be built or if existing building may be old, dilapidated, and in need of repair.

So how do you find these coveted tenants and get them to sign a legally binding contract to pay rent in a building that may not exist yet or is in need of significant rehab or repair?

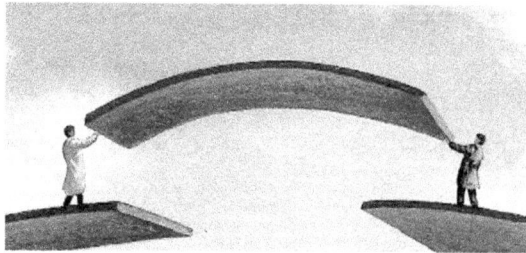

CHAPTER 3: THE GOLDEN RULE OF REAL ESTATE

INTRODUCTION

In chapter one, we pointed out that there is a fundamental component that stretches across each of the major areas of the development process. This fundamental component is money. All development projects need money. Since development projects can be expensive, most developers look to third parties such as commercial banks and investors to supply the money needed to finance the development project. In chapter two, we focused on the fact that the single most important factor to lenders and investors to finance a development project is the belief that they will get paid back. The most reliable way to prove to investors that they will get paid back is to attract rent-paying quality tenants to the project who have signed a long-term lease. However, as we pointed out before, getting a tenant to sign a long-term lease is not that easy when the building(s) is not yet built or may be in poor condition.

So how do you find these coveted tenants and get them to sign a legally binding contract to pay rent in a building that doesn't exist yet or is in bad shape?

1 LOCATION, LOCATION, LOCATION

Often the fundamental component to attracting prospective tenants to a development project is location. The generally accepted mantra for putting a real estate project on the right track for success is location, location, location. Pick up any article about real estate, look at any website, or watch any show on television today and you will find that most real estate decisions are based on location. Location is probably the single most important factor for attracting and retaining tenants, especially desirable, financially stable tenants.

2 TENANTS AND LOCATION

Site selection or location should help the developer focus on the key benefits to the tenant. The surrounding demographic and market information should strongly support the new project. Focus on the location and the location information most important to the tenant and the tenant's trade or business, and getting them to sign a long-term lease agreement will be much easier.

3 OTHER DEVELOPMENT PRODUCT TYPES

There are some commercial property development types that traditionally do not prelease. This author refers to these product types as the "build it and they will come" variety. The most common example of this is the typical apartment complex, or what is often referred to as multifamily development. Since apartment developments typically do not prelease, the developer will need to demonstrate to the financing partners and others that the location is ideal, demand is overwhelming, and comparable multifamily apartments in the area leased up quickly. Of course, the developer may also need to show a significant track record of success in the product and surrounding area and that there is a large, eager pool of buyers for the product once completed. In more difficult markets this type of product, the "build it and they will come" variety, will often require that the developer secure a guaranteed take out of the construction lender at the time the loan matures.

SUMMARY

The golden rule of real estate, location, location, location, might well be translated to *finance, finance, finance.* If developers can finance a project, they can get it built or renovated. The best way to convince a lender to lend and an investor to invest (the financing) is to sign up high-quality tenants to a long-term lease. Of course, it's not always easy to sign up high-quality tenants to a long-term lease. The easiest way to sign up coveted tenants to your development or investment effort is to secure the most attractive location for their trade and business. ➡ *Simply said, location attracts tenants, tenants pay rent, and rent-paying tenants attract financing.* The three key components of successful commercial real estate development are good location, rent-paying tenants, and money, or *financing.* It's that simple.

SECTION 2:
CAN THE PROJECT MAKE MONEY?

10 SIMPLE STEPS

In this section:

Ten Simple Steps to Determine if a Commercial Real Estate

Project is Financially Feasible

INTRODUCTION

So how do you get started? How does the developer take the information related to the three keys to developing commercial real estate—financing, tenants, and location—and answer the simple question: can the project make money? As you might have already guessed, there is one thing that simplifies this entire process, the key to successful development of commercial real estate—TENANTS. If you have an indication of interest, letter of intent, or signed lease agreement from a tenant or mix of tenants, you are well on your way to a successful commercial real estate project. Remember, tenants pay rent, rent creates cash flow, and predictable cash flow creates value.

Of course, there are some commercial development product types that traditionally don't "prelease"; multifamily or apartments are a good example. This type of product is what this author refers to as the "build it and they will come" variety. For this type of commercial real estate project, the developer must do some initial design and development work and estimate some key features and benefits. For example, to estimate potential revenue of a planned multifamily development, you will need to know the number of apartment units and unit types or mix. The unit types or mix refers to number of bedrooms and baths and how many of each might be contemplated for the overall development. This will help you estimate the revenue per unit and ultimately allow you to estimate an average price per foot for the total rentable square footage. Moreover you will to do a lot of market research related to demand for apartments and research related to comparable apartments in the market, more about this later in the chapter.

So how does a developer take all the material variables and assumptions that must be considered in developing a commercial real estate project and determine if a project might be feasible, can make money, and be a success? This chapter of the book will help guide you in analyzing each step of the process by outlining the key assumptions and using a simple format to help determine if the project can make money. In order to address the simple question of whether the project can make money, the developer should address five basic financially related issues: rent or lease revenue, value of the project when sold, total project cost, financing cost, and, finally, profit.

CHAPTER 4: ESTIMATING PROJECT RENT OR LEASE REVENUE

INTRODUCTION

Let's assume you know the lead doctor for a large medical group, and she has told you they are looking to open a new surgery center near the local medical center. She has indicated a need for no less than fifty thousand *square feet* for the new surgery center complex (ASSUMPTION #1). You tell her you have a land site in mind on an active, visible corner and adjacent to the local medical center (if you don't know of a piece of land, this would be a good time to go find one!). You explain to her that the current market for medical lease space in the area is around twenty dollars per foot in *base rent*, triple net (ASSUMPTION #2). *Triple net (NNN)* means tenant will pay their proportionate share of property taxes, maintenance, and insurance. Tenants' proportionate share of expenses just refers to how much space they are leasing compared to how much space is leased in the entire building.

Let's assume further that the doctor indicates to you that the base rent amount might be within her budget, but she would need at least thirty dollars per foot in *tenant improvement* or *"TI allowance"* from the landlord (ASSUMPTION #3). TI allowance is landlord- or developer-funded cost to make the lease space suitable for the tenant's business. Finally you indicate that thirty dollars TI allowance seems fair, but in light of this substantial landlord investment in the tenant space, you feel the lease term will need to be for no less than ten years (ASSUMPTION #4).

LEASE REVENUE ANALYSIS

Believe it or not, you now have enough information to see if the project makes financial sense. Moreover you now know the key assumptions, so even if the potential surgery center client had not told you all of the above information, you can estimate some of the assumptions and still complete an estimate. If you are developing a commercial project type that typically does not prelease, you will have to rely on the information you can collect studying the comparable projects in the location you want to build. Comparable in this case means similar. In order to determine estimated gross revenue for this type of commercial project, you will need to know the total square rentable footage you propose to build and the average lease rates you propose to charge. This information can be found by studying the comparable commercial projects that already exist in the market—more about this concept later in this chapter.

Here is how you can utilize the surgery center information to do a quick financial "snapshot" of whether the project can make money.

ESTIMATING *PROJECT REVENUE* — SIMPLE ANALYSIS

STEP ONE: ESTIMATE ANNUAL RENTAL REVENUE - Twenty dollars per foot (triple net lease) over 50,000 square feet is equal to one million dollars ($20 x 50,000) in *lease revenue* or *gross rental income* per year.

STEP TWO: ESTIMATE ANNUAL NET INCOME - The experienced developer would probably discount the rental income for three things: credit risk, vacancy factor, and capital expenditures (ASSUMPTION #5). *Credit Risk* is just an assessment by the lender of the creditworthiness of the tenant—will they pay the rent as due. *Capital expenses* are expenses not typically reimbursed or covered in triple net costs paid by the tenant. Since this is a new build surgery center, let's assume a 3 percent discount for both the credit risk and capital budget. In addition, most developers will build in a *vacancy factor*; even with a single tenant, most construction lenders and equity investors often require a vacancy factor. Since the surgery center is a single tenant operator, let's assume 2 percent. So you subtract the 5 percent, or $50,000, for capital credit risk/expenses/vacancy from the $1 million for an estimated $950,000 in *net operating income*, often referred to as the "NOI" generated each year.

- Note the estimated "triple net" expenses for the building are included in the table below. As the table indicates, the triple net expenses have no real impact in the final calculation because while the developer/landlord pays these expenses, the tenant reimburses the expenses back to the developer/landlord in the form of *additional rent*. The local commercial real estate broker or seller should be able to give you a good estimate of triple net expenses for comparable buildings or projects.

SURGERY CENTER 50,000 square feet	Total	PSF
Revenue		
Annual Gross Base Rent	$1,000,000	$20
Triple Net Expense Paid by Tenant	$400,000	$8
Total Revenue	$1,400,000	$28
Expenses		
Triple Net Expenses Paid by Landlord	$400,000	$8
Cap Expenditures and Vacancy (5% of Gross Base Rent)	$50,000	$1
Net Operating Income (NOI)	**$950,000**	**$19**

In the surgery center example there is a potential tenant, and by asking the right questions you can get the information you need to project success. How do you as the developer ask and answer the questions if you are developing a product type that doesn't typically prelease like a surgery center? What do you do if you are developing a multifamily or apartment complex? Apartment complex developments rarely prelease, and the tenants are individual renters with little or no knowledge of the issues. In this instance the developer must be able to demonstrate to the potential financing partners that the demand is so great for the product type and the location so compelling that you can justify or demonstrate a substantial need and that this need justifies the investment risk.

In this type of commercial development, the golden rule of real estate might be *"comparables, comparables, comparables." Comparables* refers to product type that is clearly similar to the project you are proposing to build. If you are proposing to build apartments, you must find apartments in the surrounding area that look a lot like the apartment complex you might be proposing and that the features, benefits, and rental rates are the same or comparable to what you are planning for your project. With this information you can demonstrate to financing partners and others that since the comparable projects were successful, your project should be successful. Of course, you will also need to demonstrate that there is great demand for another project.

Chapter 5: Estimating Project Sale Value

INTRODUCTION

So we now know the estimated project rental or lease revenue and projected net operating income. Now what? How do you take this information and estimate project value when sold? How does a developer estimate the amount of money someone might pay for the project once completed? To estimate project value upon sale, most developers will utilize the *capitalization* or "*cap rate*" method of *valuation*.

CAP RATE VALUATION

Cap rates for "comparable" properties are the easiest way to estimate project value. Cap rates are merely the real estate market's way to express the *long-term value* of the project's first full year's cash flow (the NOI). The cap rate is the market's belief in the value of net cash flow for the project over the life of the lease agreement. The important thing to remember is that applying the estimated cap rate to the estimated project NOI will help you determine what someone will or should pay for the project. Yes, you can reasonably estimate the financial value upon sale for a project that may not have been built, purchased, and renovated yet.

So how do you determine the appropriate cap rate? Determining an appropriate cap rate will typically involve a few conversations with the real estate brokerage community, bankers, and equity investors as well as a little work on the Internet. The key is to find out what cap rate was used in transactions that sold that are similar to your proposed project or building. In our example, you need to know the applicable cap rate for other surgery centers that have sold—preferably in the recent past and in the same general area as your development site. If the surgery centers that sold were similar to the one you are planning to develop (or buy and refurbish) then you can reasonably expect that a future buyer will utilize the same or similar cap rate to value your project. Here is the key formula to remember:

◼️ *PROJECT VALUE = NET OPERATING INCOME/CAP RATE*

ESTIMATING PROJECT VALUE

STEP THREE: DETERMINE THE APPROPRIATE "CAP" RATE - The developer checks the Internet and numerous local brokers and bankers and learns that three buildings located in the local medical center with large surgery clinic tenants have sold in the last few years. The cap rates from these three sales ranged from 6.5-8.5 percent. To be conservative, you decide to model an 8 percent cap rate (ASSUMPTION #6). Note: the inverse relationship between the cap rate percentage and sales value (the lower the cap rate the higher the sales value). To determine the potential sales value of the surgery center project, the developer divides the estimated NOI ($950,000) by the assumed cap rate (.08) for a total potential sales value of approximately $11,875,000.

STEP FOUR: ESTIMATE CLOSING COST - As with every deal, there are costs involved. In selling the now completed commercial real estate project, the developer may have hired a broker, or the buyer may have engaged a broker, and this will result in commission cost (more about calculating brokerage commission later in this section). If we assume 4 percent for brokerage commission, closing costs, and expenses, the *net sale price* should yield the developer $11,400,000 (ASSUMPTION #7).

SURGERY CENTER Project Sale Value	Total	PSF
Net Operating Income	$950,000	$19
Cap Rate	8.0%	
Est. Gross Sales Proceeds	$11,875,000	$237.50
Cost of Sale, including commission (4%)	($475,000)	($9.50)
Est. Net Sales Proceeds	**$11,400,000**	**$228**

- The developer now believes that if she can get the surgery center client to sign the lease agreement, get the land purchased, the building built (or purchased), and the surgery center tenant moved in and paying rent, she can reasonably expect to sell the project, after expenses, for approximately $11,400,000.

- Moreover there is one additional financial fact we have learned—a very important financial fact. The developer also knows the rent paid by the surgery center tenant will generate $79,167 a month in cash flow (annual NOI of $950,000/12). With $79,167 each month of projected rent or cash flow, the developer should be able to borrow enough to buy the land, build the building, and get the tenants moved in and paying rent. Therefore, based on the conversations with the potential tenant, brokers, bankers, and some Internet research, we now can estimate the project revenue, income, and value upon sale. That's pretty good information for one conversation with your potential surgery center tenant!

Chapter 6: Estimating Project Construction Cost

INTRODUCTION

We have now estimated the project revenue, annual NOI, a market-driven cap rate, and what the project might sell for. However, we are still missing important information. How do we know how much the project might cost? How does the developer estimate *total project cost* for a project that is probably only an idea or possibly a *construction drawing*?

THREE MAJOR CONSTRUCTION COSTS

There are three basic construction-related costs that we must consider to accurately forecast the *total project construction-related costs*. The basic construction-related costs are 1) cost of buying the land, 2) cost of getting the project designed and built, and 3) cost of getting the tenants moved in and paying rent. Of course, if you are buying an existing building, the three key items are different. If you purchase an existing building, the three basic costs are 1) cost of buying the building, 2) cost of basic rehab and repair, and 3) the cost of making the space suitable for intended tenants and users (more about the cost of purchasing and refurbishing an existing building in part three of this book).

Land Cost – Estimating the land cost should be simple enough: what is the seller's asking price? Of course, every seller wants maximum value for their land, so the developer might want to do a little homework to determine a fair price. What are some recent sales prices of similar property in the general area of the chosen site? Talk to other sellers and real estate brokers about other properties that are similar, research project sales on the Internet, and then make your best guess as to what the seller will sell the land for. Remember, everything is negotiable. As always, add some closing costs and expenses, and you probably have a good land cost estimate (no commission this time as typically the seller pays commission—more about this later in the chapter).

Construction and Design Cost – The cost of *design* and construction of the building may be less certain than the cost of the land, but it is not that difficult to estimate.

If the developer has experience with surgery centers or other similar buildings then this process is simple. The developer can use past experience to estimate design and construction cost. If you do not have prior experience developing surgery centers, you will need to talk to someone who has. Find an architect and general contractor who has this experience. An *architect* and *general contractor* experienced in surgery center design and construction should be able to give you cost estimates to design and build a 50,000-square-foot surgery center. In addition, the architect and general contractor can give you estimates on other important items such as how long it should take to design, permit, and build the project. In the previous section we found three similar projects that sold in the past few years. These projects might be good cost models for estimating the cost and timing of the project. Find out who designed and built the comparable centers and discuss with them your project and you should be well on your way to getting good estimates for your own project.

Tenant Improvement and Lease Commission – In addition to land, design, and construction cost we need to estimate how much it will cost the developer to get the tenant moved into the project. Almost every tenant needs some specific build out before they move in. It is common in most markets for the landlord to pay some portion of these specific build-out costs, referred to as *tenant improvement costs* or *landlord tenant improvement allowance*, or "TI." Remember, once the building is built and tenants have moved in, you are also now known as the landlord. The local real estate broker can help you estimate the typical tenant improvement amount a landlord should offer.

In our example, the doctor told us that she needed at least thirty dollars per foot in tenant improvement allowance. This amount is probably half or less than half of the total TI needed to finish out a surgery center. This means that the tenant will have to invest the remaining TI amounts needed to get the business up and running. That's a good thing—the developer, construction lender, equity investor, and potential buyers all want to see the tenant invest money into the lease space. If you plan to develop a project like an apartment complex, the benefits and features of the tenant space are typically built in and included as part of the construction hard costs. Tenants who look to lease space in an apartment complex expect the space to be *move-in* ready.

Finally, it is important to consider brokerage fees or commissions. Brokerage commissions are almost always paid by the seller and/or developer/landlord. In many instances the developer will have engaged a broker or the tenant will have engaged a broker. If there is a broker involved, you will need to account for the brokerage commission associated with the lease agreement in the overall budget. The brokerage commission can vary, but typically if both the buyer and the seller are represented by brokers, you can assume a total of 3-6 percent. The broker commission is determined by multiplying the agreed upon percent (3-6 percent) by the total estimated rent to be paid over the term of the lease (ten years for the surgery center example).

In our example you found the tenant through your own efforts, so we will assume no brokerage commission is to be paid. However, don't be surprised if the tenant introduces a broker to the transaction. Tenants often like to rely on real estate professionals to help navigate the many market issues of a long-term lease agreement. More importantly, they know that the developer/owner typically pays the brokerage commission. For purposes of calculating brokerage commission we will assume the tenant has engaged a commercial real estate broker. The calculation is shown below.

ESTIMATING PROJECT CONSTRUCTION COST

STEP FIVE: ESTIMATE COST OF THE LAND OR BUILDING - The corner parcel adjacent to the medical center you have in mind is two acres, or 87,120 square feet (**43,560 feet in one acre**), and you have shown the location to the physician and she likes it. You have talked to the seller, and the seller is asking five dollars per foot for the site. Therefore you estimate the purchase price of the land to be $435,600 (87,120 feet x $5). Since we are estimating costs, let's assume $500,000 for a total land cost because of legal and other closing costs (no brokerage commission to budget since these costs should be paid by the seller) (ASSUMPTION #8).

STEP SIX: ESTIMATE COST OF DESIGN AND CONSTRUCTION - The developer talks to a local general contractor experienced in surgery center construction, and they believe the estimated construction, or *hard costs* (actual construction cost), to be one hundred dollars per foot, or five million dollars (50,000 square feet x $100). You have also found an architect, and she estimates the total design costs, or *soft costs* (design, engineering, and fees), to be another ten dollars per foot, or $500,000 (50,000 square feet x $10) for a total estimated design and construction cost of $5.5 million (ASSUMPTION #9).

STEP SEVEN: ADD A DEVELOPER FEE - A developer fee is one way you get paid for all of your efforts. The developer fee can vary dramatically, but it is typically in the range of 3-6 percent of total development cost. In this case let's assume you add another ten dollars per foot, or $500,000, to the soft cost budget to cover *developer fee and other contingencies* (ASSUMPTION #10).

STEP EIGHT: ESTIMATE TENANT IMPROVEMENT COST AND BROKERAGE COMMISSION - Remember the doctor told us she needed thirty dollars per foot in owner or landlord TI allowance, or $1.5 million ($30 x 50,000 square feet). In addition, let's also assume the tenant has engaged a real estate broker to help negotiate the deal, and you negotiated a 2 percent commission (ASSUMPTION #11). The brokerage commission for a lease agreement is calculated on total revenue during the initial term of the lease. In the surgery center example, we have $1 million in revenue or gross lease payments each year for ten years, or $10 million. If you take this amount times 4 percent, you get $400,000 for the lease commission to the broker. There are also commissions that may be payable if the lease renews or extends, and in some markets brokerage commission can be payable on additional rent amounts like triple net reimbursements. In any event it is important to understand the impact brokerage commissions might have on the project profitability.

SURGERY CENTER Design and Construction Cost	Total	PSF
2 Acre Land Cost (plus closing cost)	$500,000	$5.74 per acre ft.
Design and Construction Cost	$5,500,000	$110
Developer Fee and Costs	$500,000	$10
Tenant Improvement Cost	$1,500,000	$30
Brokerage Commission	$400,000	$8
Total Project Construction Cost	**$8,400,000**	**$168**

You have now estimated annual and monthly revenue, projected NOI, appropriate cap rate, possible value of the project if sold, and the cost of the three key construction items: land cost, building design and construction cost, and tenant improvement cost (and brokerage commission). Now what? With the current information, it appears that the project can be profitable. We have estimated our total construction cost at $8.4 million and our sale price at $11.4 million, leaving a potential profit of $3 million. However, there is one additional very important cost to consider—the cost of borrowing the money to buy the land, design and construct the project, and get the tenants moved in and paying rent.

Chapter 7: Estimating Project Construction Loan Cost

INTRODUCTION

There is one additional cost to consider, one very important cost—the cost of borrowing the money needed to complete the project. ◄ Remember, all commercial real estate projects take money—the financing. The financing is typically in the form of a construction loan. How does the developer estimate the cost of borrowing the money to buy the land, build the building, and get the tenants moved in and paying rent?

CONSTRUCTION LOAN — DEBT SERVICE COVERAGE RATIO

Construction lenders apply numerous *underwriting* criteria in making a construction real estate loan. Underwriting just refers to the homework or diligence lenders perform when considering a loan application. One of these underwriting criteria is to require that the projected annual or monthly cash flow from the project cover the anticipated debt service of the loan. Most construction lenders will require no less than a 1.2 *debt service coverage ratio* ("*DSCR*") to make a construction loan to a commercial real estate development project. The DSCR is just a complicated way to say that the project monthly *net cash flow* ($79,167) must be at least 1.2 times the presumed or estimated monthly mortgage payment. To determine the minimum required DSCR, the developer divides this monthly NOI by the 1.2 (or whatever minimum the bank might require).

In our case the discounted NOI at a 1.2 DSCR would be $65,972, or $79,167/1.2. The $65,972 represents the monthly loan payment the lender believes the developer can reasonably support each month without creating too much stress on the project cash flow (or more importantly bank management). ◄ Most lenders base their DSCR on a combined principal and interest payment. This means that in order to determine the DSCR, the construction lender will look at the loan, or *underwrite* the loan, as if they are the long-term lender. In reality the construction lender is only the short-term lender.

Construction loans are usually only outstanding for the time it takes to build the building and get the tenants moved in, and then the loan must be refinanced or sold. However, construction lenders will determine the DSCR as if they were the permanent lender. The reason for this is obvious—if they do become the permanent lender, they need to know that there is enough monthly cash flow to make the mortgage payments. Moreover, most construction lenders will offer, in conjunction with the construction loan, financing a loan that can be used to take out the construction loan, often referred to as a *mini perm*. The mini perm converts the construction loan to a fully amortizable loan of both interest and principal over a short term (five to ten years).

CONSTRUCTION LOAN — INTEREST ONLY

As mentioned, commercial real estate construction loans are typically structured as interest only for the construction period and then must be refinanced or converted to a more *permanent loan* type. After the interest-only period has expired, the interest rate and payment will either adjust to fully amortize over a longer period or the loan must be paid off from another source—such as the mini perm mentioned above or proceeds from the sale of the development project. To estimate construction loan cost, the developer must find out under what terms a bank might lend the money needed on a longer-term basis. So let's assume you visit with your local banker(s) and believe a bank will agree to a twenty-year loan and will fix the interest rate at 5 percent and allow you to make interest-only payments for three years. Finally, the general contractor believes the estimated time of construction is eighteen months.

Now we must determine the total amount of interest you must budget before the project cash flow is sufficient to make payments. How much money do you need to borrow before the project cash flow takes over the interest payments to the lender? Once you determine how much interest is needed, you add this amount to the $8.4 million to determine our estimated total project cost.

CONSTRUCTION LOAN — LOAN TO COST AND LOAN TO VALUE LIMITATIONS

Commercial real estate construction lenders have numerous ways to help ensure that the loan will be repaid. Requiring long-term lease agreements signed with quality tenants is one way. However, there are numerous other ways banks structure real estate loans to increase the chances they will get paid back. We have already discussed the

DSCR concept. However, there are two other construction loan concepts important for the developer to understand, especially if you are attempting to estimate total project cost—*loan to cost* and *loan to value* limitations.

"Loan to cost" is how much the construction lender will lend based on estimated total project cost while "loan to value" is how much a lender will lend based on the projected value at sale. How does the developer determine whether a lender will utilize a loan-to-value or a loan-to-cost methodology? Yes, you guessed it—does the developer have a long-term lease agreement signed by a quality tenant for all or a majority of the leasable space? If the developer has a lease agreement signed by a quality tenant, the lender can reasonably estimate cash flow (rent). Cash flow means you will have the ability to make loan payments. Cash flow means there will likely be a buyer or refinance options when the loan matures. Typically you can expect a construction lender to lend 65-80 percent of project cost regardless of whether they utilize the cost or valuation method. Ultimately the lender will commission an *appraisal* to determine project value and therefore how much the lender will lend. Don't underestimate the importance of the appraisal. The bank will hire a third-party professional *appraiser* who will do a study related to the property and issue a property value using several appraisal methods.

In our example, we are assuming we will have a lease agreement signed by an established, reputable surgery center organization. The lease agreement will reflect strong monthly cash flow. Therefore let's assume that a lender will lend 80 percent of the estimated total project cost (ASSUMPTION #12). Of course, if the construction lender will only lend 80 percent of projected cost, there will not be enough money to complete the project. Now what? Where does the additional money come from? The additional money is often referred to as the project equity—more about the project equity in the next section of this chapter. One final note about construction lenders: outlined in this chapter are numerous ways the lender gets comfortable that the loan is a good one. However, there are many other loan requirements that also add to this comfort level that have not been addressed above, not the least of which is the *developer guarantee* of the construction loan. Yes, you will be asked to *guarantee* the loan!

ESTIMATING COST OF THE CONSTRUCTION LOAN

STEP NINE: ESTIMATE COST OF THE CONSTRUCTION LOAN – Let's assume you met with a banker and he or she told you, based on what you told him or her, that the project would appear to support a construction loan for 80 percent of the estimated cost at a 5 percent fixed rate, with interest-only payments for three years and will lend as part of the construction loan the interest needed during the estimated construction period of eighteen months (ASSUMPTION #13).

With this information from the banker, how does the developer estimate the interest to be paid during the construction? At this point you could use a mortgage calculator, financial model, or even a compound interest table. The good news is that *mortgage calculators*, financial models, and compound interest rate tables can all easily be found on the Internet. However, for the nonfinancial type of developer, outlined below is a simple method to estimate the interest payment.

Remember, construction loans are funded monthly, as you need the money to buy and build. Therefore the loans are not really fully funded until the end of construction. Because of this, the *average outstanding principal balance* at any point in time can be difficult to estimate for purposes of calculating the total interest to be paid during the course of construction. In order to simplify this estimate, some developers will utilize a financial "shortcut." Here is how it works:

Take the estimated total project cost of $8.4 million (land, design and construction, TI, and brokerage commission and fees) and then apply the loan terms that the banker outlined to you in the earlier conversation:

1. Estimated total project cost ($8.4 million) x loan-to-cost limitation (80 percent) x 50 percent x interest rate (5 percent) x construction period of eighteen months or 1.5 years.

Note: the only thing we added to the banker's information was the 50 percent. The 50 percent represents an easy way to reflect the average estimated outstanding loan balance. The 50 percent creates a simple outstanding principal balance and helps make the estimation easier.

2. $8,400,000 x 80% x 50% x 5% x 1.5;

   $8,400,000 x (80%) = $6,720,000

   $6,720,000 (50%) = $3,360,000

   $3,360,000 (5%) = $168,000

   $168,000 (18 months or 1.5) = $252,000

Based on these assumptions, it appears that we can estimate the total interest we need to borrow to be $252,000. Since we know there will be some costs involved (loan fees, title policy, legal, etc.), let's increase this amount to $300,000. The $300,000 represents the estimated total amount of interest we need to pay the bank during the construction period before the cash flow from the project becomes sufficient to make the interest payment. The developer must now add the $300,000 to the overall cost estimate to determine the amount we need to borrow.

SURGERY CENTER Total Project Cost	Total	PSF
Total Project Construction Cost	$8,400,000	$168
Construction Interest and Expenses	$300,000	$6
Total Project Cost	$8,700,000	$174
80% Loan-to-Cost Limitation	$6,960,000	$139
Amount of Money Still Needed to Construct	$1,740,000	$35

Chapter 8: The Equity Investor and Estimating Project Profit

INTRODUCTION

As demonstrated from the chart in the prior section and described in the loan to value paragraph, the construction lender is only willing to lend 80 percent of total development cost. This means the developer still needs an additional $1,740,000 ($8,700,000 − $6,960,000 = $1,740,000) to complete the project. This additional money is often referred to as equity. Project equity can come from many sources. The equity might very well be the land the project is to be built on or cash invested by friends, other banks, or investment firms. Of course, if you have the capability, equity can always come from you, the developer. No matter where it comes from, you almost always need some additional money to complement the construction loan. Equity can also come in the form of a *mezzanine or subordinated loan (subordinated to the construction lender). The additional loan is used* to help bridge the difference between the debt and the money needed to complete the project.

THE EQUITY INVESTOR

There are typically two parts to the total cost of borrowing the money needed to build a new project—the construction loan and the equity investment. Equity investment can come from many sources, but regardless of the source, equity investors typically require the following approach to their investment: a *rate return* or *preferred return* on the invested money, the return of all money invested, or the invested principal and a large percentage of the profit from the project. This concept is important because ultimately what you pay the equity investor will reduce the overall return to you, the developer.

The interest rate component payable to the equity investor is not typically paid current each month like the construction lender (at least not in the early stages of the project) but paid upon the sale or *refinance* of the project. Because the interest rate is not paid current, the interest on the preferred return will often be compounded. *Compounding interest* just means the previous year's earned interest will be added to the outstanding principal in determining the next year's interest earned, and this is done for each year the investment is outstanding.

As mentioned earlier, you can utilize a *compound interest rate table* to determine the appropriate multiplier that corresponds to the period of time and interest rate for the specific investment. Once you know the multiplier, you then multiply that by the initial investment amount to derive the potential or future value of the investment. Finally, the project equity investor will typically expect the developer to put up 5-10 percent of the total equity investment needed. This is often referred to as *skin in the game* or the *developer co-investment. The good news is that the developer will also get a preferred return on his or her investment, the return of money invested, and finally a percentage of the profit.*

To determine the overall *return on investment*, or *ROI*, that an equity investor will require, we must find out the typical terms required by investors for investments in real estate projects like this one. The developer can get this information by talking to different equity investment groups, bankers, real estate brokers, or other developers. Once we have gathered this information, the developer can determine the cost of the equity investment.

INTRODUCTION

In the prior sections, the developer estimated the total project cost by calculating the three basic construction-related costs and the cost to borrow the money needed to complete the project. You can now calculate the project potential profit by subtracting the total project cost from the presumed proceeds from selling the project to determine estimated project profit.

PROJECT PROFIT

The developer now believes the total project cost including construction loan interest cost to be $8.7 million. Moreover, you believe the project can be sold at an 8 percent cap rate yielding $11.4 million (net of sales cost). Therefore the developer can reasonably anticipate that if all goes well and you are successful getting the lease signed, land purchased, loan closed, project built, and tenant moved in and paying rent that the project can be successful. The project appears capable of yielding a good profit for both the equity investor and the developer. Thus this project appears feasible and should make money.

DISTRIBUTION OF PROFIT

It appears the project can be profitable, and if everything goes according to plan, the net profit is estimated to be $2.7 million. Unfortunately, you don't get to keep all of the profit. The developer must pay the investment partners or equity investors. As mentioned previously, the equity investors (including you as the developer if you put in equity capital) will typically receive an interest rate return on the money invested and all their invested money or principal back, and the remaining profit would be split as agreed in the original investment agreement between the developer and equity investors.

STEP TEN: ESTIMATE PROJECT PROFIT AND CASH TO INVESTORS - With the new total project cost estimate of $8.7 million, we must now determine how much we can borrow. Since we know the bank will only fund 80 percent of total project cost, we can determine that the lender will only let us borrow $6,960,000 ($8,700,000 x 80 percent). Since we can only borrow $6,960,000, we know we need additional money or equity in the amount of $1,740,000 ($8,700,000 - $6,960,000).

So let's assume the equity investor agreed to an 8 percent compounded interest rate, or "pref," on their money. The money will be invested for three years and no interest will be paid during this time (ASSUMPTION #14). A quick search on the Internet will locate a compounded interest rate table. The multiplier for a three-year investment at 8 percent compounded interest is 1.2597. To determine the preferred interest payment to the equity investors once the project is sold we must apply the multiplier to the original investment amount to determine the increased value of the original investment and then calculate the difference:

1. $1,740,000 (original equity investment) x 1.2597 (multiplier) = $2,191,878
2. $1,740,000 - $2,191,878 = $451,878
3. $451,878 rounded up to $455,000 in projected interest payable to the equity investor (don't forget we are estimating so rounding assumed figures can make the job easier).

So if we now assume the project is built and sold as planned, we will have $10,950,000 (net of cost of sale) in gross sale proceeds. We must first pay back the construction loan principal amount of $6,740,000. This leaves the developer with $4,210,000 in *net distributable proceeds*, sometimes referred to as the cash "waterfall." We must then pay the equity investors their accumulated preferred interest payments of $455,000 and pay back the original money or equity invested of $1,740,000. Once you make these payments, you are left with the project net profit, or what is often referred to as the, *promote* in the amount of $2,015,000 ($4,210,000 – $455,000 – $1,740,000). This amount then gets distributed between the developer and the equity investors depending on the original arrangement in the investment documents.

SURGERY CENTER Construction Cost	Total	PSF
Net Operating Income	$950,000	$19
Cap Rate	8.0%	
Gross Sale Proceeds	$11,875,000	$237.50
Costs of Sale	$475,000	$9.50
Net Sale Proceeds	$10,950,000	$219
Current Loan	$6,740,000	$135
Net Distributable Proceeds	$4,210,000	$84
1) Preferred Return to Equity	**($455,000)**	$10
2) Return of Principal Invested	**($1,740,000)**	$34.80
3) Amount of Profit of		
Promote	**$2,015,000**	$40.30

Based on the financial estimates and projections set forth above for this project, it appears that the equity investor and the developer can reasonably expect to get an 8 percent "pref" on their money, get their money back, and then split a profit of more than $2 million!

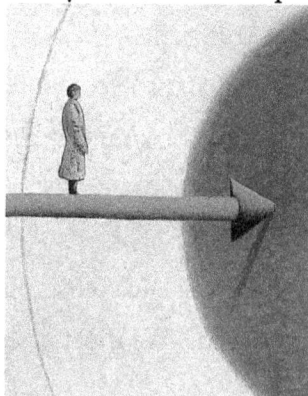

SECTION 3:
HOW TO PURCHASE AND REHAB AN EXISTING COMMERCIAL BUILDING

In this section:

How to Purchase and Rehab an Existing Commercial Real Estate Property – What Are the Costs and Risks?

INTRODUCTION

So let's assume there is a specific commercial real estate building or project you would like to purchase. The building or commercial project is in a good location but has been empty and in disrepair for a few years. The location of the site is close to a major medical center, and you think the building, once purchased and *rehabbed*, can appeal to medically related tenants and users. The objective in purchasing the building is to buy it, fix it up, lease the space to new medical tenants, and then sell the stabilized building for a profit.

So how do you analyze the true cost of purchasing an existing commercial building or project? The true cost of purchasing an existing commercial building is more than the purchase price. The true cost of purchasing an existing building or project not only includes the purchase price but the cost of rehabbing and repairing the building and making the building suitable and attractive for the intended tenant and users. In analyzing the purchase of an existing commercial building, the basic principles of this book still apply. ◄ Attracting rent-paying tenants remains the most important aspect of any commercial real estate development, whether it's a new building or existing commercial building. Once the developer has tenants interested in leasing in the building, finding the financing to purchase and rehab will be much easier. So how does a developer reasonably assess and analyze the true "all in" cost of purchasing an existing commercial building or project?

CHAPTER 9: FIVE MAJOR COSTS IN PURCHASING AND REHABBING AN EXISTING BUILDING

There are five major cost issues that you must address to assess the overall investment in purchasing and rehabbing an existing commercial building. These are: 1) the purchase price of the building, 2) the cost of basic rehabilitation and repair, 3) the cost to make the space suitable for the intended tenants and users, 4) the tenant improvement cost or landlord tenant improvement allowance, and 5) the real estate brokerage commissions. Understanding these five costs will help you evaluate the real cost of acquiring the project and determine if the investment makes good economic sense. Ultimately the overall investment must make good economic sense; translate to competitive lease terms for the intended tenants and an attractive return for you and your investors.

PURCHASING THE PROJECT OR BUILDING

If you own an existing commercial building and want to sell it, you probably want the highest possible price. Of course if you are the buyer, you likely have a very different perspective. The price that an existing commercial real estate project sells for is almost always subject to negotiation. From the seller's perspective, the single most important factor in asking for a high price is typically the cash flow generated from tenants. However, if you are selling an older building in need of repair, location might be the value creator. Location is important to sales price or perceived value because location is often the single most important factor for attracting tenants and users.

Buyers have a similar perspective but for different reasons. Buyers have a similar perspective because they to want to attract tenants and users to the site. However, buyers want the lowest possible purchase price so they can offer attractive terms to the all-important tenants (or another buyer) and still make a profit. One very important way to determine a fair or market-driven price is to find out what other comparable properties in the surrounding area have sold for. In addition, knowing the current asking price from other sellers for comparable properties in the surrounding area can also be helpful in determining a fair price. If you are considering the purchase of an existing building, you can always use the seller's asking price for purposes of financial modeling or estimating cost.

MAJOR REHABILITATION AND REPAIR COST

Let's assume you have decided on an initial estimate for the purchase of the building or project. Now what? With an estimated purchase price you can now focus on the other important cost items. Most tenants will require you to deliver a building that meets certain minimum standards: good *foundation*, solid walls, leak-free roof, *HVAC* systems working, utilities to the site and working, dependable mechanical systems, no environmental issues, and a building that generally meets local codes and requirements. With this in mind, the first cost item you should focus on is the estimated cost of major rehab/repair. Keep in mind you are early in the process and probably do not yet have a letter of intent or purchase contract. You are merely trying to make an initial assessment or best guess of the total cost of purchasing the building. To adequately evaluate, the developer must make an *initial inspection* of the project and surrounding area. Initial inspections are great ways to learn a lot about the building and basic issues. As a buyer, you can learn a lot walking through the building just turning things on and off and looking for obvious signs of problems or issues.

The goal of the initial inspections should be to identify the major issues that will make the rehab project more expensive or extremely difficult or time consuming. An initial inspection can be as simple or as complex as you choose, but it should include, at a minimum, a walk-through of the property and surrounding area and a simple review of all major structures and systems, including but not limited to mechanical/electrical and plumbing as well as foundation, walls, and roof—more about the specifics of what to look for and inspect later in this chapter.

At this stage of the project you may not be ready to pay professionals to perform inspections. However, you get valuable information by asking the various professionals to look at the building and systems and give an estimate and bid on the cost of performing any needed work. Most professionals asked to make an initial assessment for purposes of submitting a bid to perform work will offer observations while walking the building or bidding on the work. This means it is a good idea for you to be present when they are at the building. For example, an environmental inspector who you ask to give a bid on doing an "*Environmental Phase I*" report will often identify issues as he or she walks through the building, such as floor tiles, insulation, doors, or duct work that may or are likely to contain *asbestos*-related material or even areas of potential problems like roof leakage and *mold*. If this appears to be extensive, the issue can influence key points in the buying or pricing negotiations with the seller. Finally, if the building or project has a regular maintenance person, get to know him or her and try to walk the building with him or her numerous times. Often he or she has great insight into issues related to current and past problems. The maintenance person may even be someone you attempt to keep with the building if you close on the purchase.

Let's assume you have made an initial inspection and have toured the building with various professionals and want to keep moving forward with the deal. To complete the assessment, the developer must still consider a few other key cost issues. These include making the space suitable for potential tenants, landlord tenant improvement allowance, and real estate brokerage commissions.

MAKING THE LEASE SPACE SUITABLE FOR TENANTS AND USERS

The true cost of purchasing an existing building includes not only the purchase price and cost of rehab and repair of the building(s) but also making the building suitable for the intended tenants and users. Making the project suitable for tenants represents costs that the developer may need to incur to attract the targeted tenants. However, these costs may not be investments that are tied directly to any specific tenant or user. For example, health-care-oriented buildings often require a covering, or "*porte cochere*," for patient drop-off and pickup. Although the cost of this feature may be allocable to the tenants, as *common area expense* it is typically a feature health-care tenants look for when shopping for space and not an expense tied to getting a specific tenant moved into the building. Moreover, the porte cochere is often a *regulatory requirement* for health-care-related buildings. Benefits and features required because of a specific use, like health care, are not only important to attract tenants but often a regulatory requirement.

If you are looking to purchase and rehab an existing building for medical use or any other commercially specific use, it is important to understand requirements of the intended tenants and users like the porte cochere. To further the example, medical buildings can require larger elevators, wider doors and hallways, handicap-accessible bathrooms, windows in every patient room, and other unique features. Many of these features may be direct costs to the developer and not associated with any specific tenant or lease.

TENANT IMPROVEMENT COSTS

Tenant improvement costs is the amount of money the landlord (you) will give to tenants in order to build out their space to make the space suitable for their business or use. A tenant improvement cost is also money you offer to entice tenants to the building. Tenant improvement cost, or what is often referred to as the landlord "*TI allowance*," can be very expensive and add substantial investment to a project. The local broker should know what the typical tenant improvement allowance is for comparable buildings in the area. Knowing what is typical in the market can be helpful for estimating what you should budget for this cost. Ultimately, however, the developer and tenant will negotiate the amount of TI to be paid by the landlord. The landlord's TI allowance is typically only a portion of the overall cost needed to build out the tenant space. The tenant is generally liable for the remaining cost needed to make the space suitable.

Of course, in our example, the developer is purchasing an existing commercial building, and some tenant space may already exist. Existing tenant build-out and space is often referred to as "second generation" space. *Second generation space* is space that is already built out for the previous user. This existing build-out may be one of the reasons a tenant is attracted to the building. Second generation space can save a developer time and money in the race to attract tenants and get the tenant moved in to the project and paying rent.

REAL ESTATE BROKERAGE COMMISSION COSTS

Finally, it is important to budget *brokerage fees* or *commissions*. In many instances you will have engaged a broker or the tenant will have engaged a broker to help negotiate the lease terms. If there is a broker engaged in the leasing process, in most markets you are expected to pay the brokerage commission for both your broker and the tenant broker. The brokerage commission will vary, but typically if the developer and the tenant are represented by brokers, you can assume a total commission of between 4 percent and 8 percent. The broker commission is normally determined by multiplying the agreed-upon real estate commission percentage by the total estimated lease payments over the length of the lease. Brokerage commission for a lease agreement can easily run into hundreds of thousands of dollars, so it is very important for the developer to budget and plan for this payment. One-half of the commission is typically paid upon signing the lease agreement or loan closing and the remaining amount is paid once the tenant moves into the building and begins to pay rent.

One final point: brokerage commission is almost always negotiable. Don't hesitate to bring up the cost or timing of the payment of the brokerage commission to the seller or the potential tenant if the deal economics are challenged. However, this is a double-edged sword as the broker is likely showing other sites to the tenant. Reduced commission could result in reduced focus by the broker on your site to the potential tenant in favor of another building or commercial real estate project.

THE COST OF BORROWING THE MONEY

As you may recall, in the very first section and chapter of this book we discussed a single component that stretched across all the key areas of developing commercial real estate. This single component is *money*. All development projects need money. One must acquire the building, pay for certain upfront costs, pay to get the project repaired and rehabbed, and pay to support the building while finding enough tenants to fill it. Since commercial real estate developments are expensive, most developers will try to borrow most of the money needed. Borrowing money for a commercial development project, even the purchase and rehab of an existing building, can be done in the form of a *bank or construction loan*. Bank or construction loans are typically short term, interest only during the term and only constitute a percentage of the total cost needed to purchase and finish the project.

Because construction loans are typically only a percentage of the cash needed (50–80 percent), you will need to find or invest additional money over and above the bank or construction loan. This additional money is often referred to as equity. The *equity investment* to make up the difference in the amount needed to complete the project can come from many sources—including you if you have the cash. Of course, from the developer's perspective we just added one more big cost to the overall project, the cost to borrow the money and obtain the additional equity investment needed to cover the estimated total costs. Borrowing the money needed to purchase, rehab/repair, and make the building suitable for tenants can add substantial cost to the project. To accurately forecast the true investment cost for purchasing an existing commercial building, you must account for all the costs of the project, including the cost of borrowing the money. See part two of this book for putting together a simple investment pro forma and estimating the total amount of money needed, including the financing.

CAN THE PROJECT MAKE MONEY?

Ultimately the developer must determine that the project is *feasible*. As mentioned earlier, the total cost of the project must still translate to lease terms that will be attractive to the tenants and result in a good return for the developer and his investors. This evaluation will often result in a negotiation with the seller to reduce the asking price. Having the results of the initial inspection, required benefits and features needed to attract tenants, landlord-estimated TI expense, brokerage commission, and cost of borrowing the money can go a long way in convincing the seller that a reduced price is justified. With the estimated total cost in hand, a revised financial plan, and possibly a reduced purchase price, you must now decide whether or not to move forward with the purchase of the project. If the decision is to move forward, the next step is to finalize a letter of intent or purchase contract with the seller.

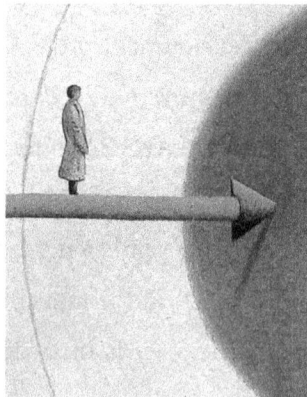

Chapter 10: Securing the Purchase of the Project

THE *LETTER OF INTENT*

Let's assume you have decided to make an offer to purchase an existing commercial building from the seller. In light of this, you would like to negotiate a letter of intent, or "LOI," before you put a purchase contract in front of the owner. Why would you want to do an LOI and not just go straight to a purchase contract? There are numerous benefits to getting a letter of intent done before you negotiate the actual contract. First, an LOI does not typically require earnest money and helps get both parties comfortable; there is a "meeting of the minds" as to the deal terms. In addition, an LOI can result in other benefits, such as getting the owner to take the building off the market for a few days or conversely help buy you more time to consider other properties. Finally, an LOI may result in more time to conduct due diligence on the building or property. Moreover, having a signed LOI to purchase the project or building can give potential tenants, equity investors, construction lenders, and teaming partners some comfort and confidence that you have the ability to get a deal done.

In addition, the LOI will contain many of the key terms that are typically set forth in a purchase contract. This can expedite getting the contract finalized, signed, and into the title company. In most instances your broker or legal counsel can supply the form of LOI and the typical provisions addressed in the letter.

Listed below are some of the key issues typically addressed in an LOI to purchase an existing commercial real project or building:

Property Location and Description

Identification *of the Buyer and Seller*

Purchase Price

Earnest Money Deposit, *additional deposit for extension of time, and special terms*

Due Diligence: definition of the feasibility or due diligence period and possible extensions

Finance Terms: *seller financing terms, assumable financing, or buyer obtaining financing*

Closing Contingencies: *identification and timing of removal of contingency items such as receipt of acceptable* **appraisal**, *proper zoning or zoning change, platting and/or permitting, cost of due diligence and identification of responsibility and cost to buyer and seller*

Disclosures: *seller disclosures such as easements, leases, restrictions, and other conditions*

Selection and identification of the **title company**

Escrow (monetary deposit): escrow instructions

Brokers: buyer and seller brokers identified and how they are to be paid

Confidentiality *provisions*

So you believe the building will work for the tenants and users you are negotiating with or hope to attract and decide to enter into a simple LOI with the seller. Now you must put the commercial building or project "*under contract.*"

THE REAL ESTATE PURCHASE AND SALE AGREEMENT

The *real estate purchase and sale agreement*, or *PSA*, is an agreement or contract between you and the seller that gives you the right but not the obligation to purchase the property or building. To enter into a purchase agreement, you and the seller (and real estate brokers, if applicable) will negotiate the basic terms and conditions under which the buildings or project can be purchased, including, of course, the purchase price. The terms and conditions should include the terms set forth above for the LOI.

As you can see, there are numerous important issues to be set forth in the PSA. One of the important items that must be negotiated is the amount of *earnest money* the developer will put up to "hold" the project. The amount of money required to hold the deal or put the deal under contract is negotiable but is typically determined by a percentage of the overall purchase price (10 percent in many markets). The earnest money is typically refundable if the buyer decides not to close on purchasing the property. If you do close on the project property, the initial earnest money should be considered a down payment and applied to reduce the purchase price at closing.

One of the other important issues you will negotiate when entering into a contract is the period of time the developer will have to conduct diligence. *Diligence* is the process and procedure to determine if the project will make sense for your intended use. This period of time to conduct diligence is often referred to as the *feasibility period.* The feasibility period means what it says—the developer has a limited period of time to determine if the purchase of the project is "feasible" for the intended use and tenants. At the end of the time period, the developer must close on the purchase of the property, walk away (with his or her earnest money), or put up additional earnest money to extend the feasibility period.

In most instances the buyer and seller will negotiate options to extend the feasibility period. Exercise of the option extensions typically requires additional earnest money and negotiations between buyer and seller whether the additional earnest money is refundable or even applicable to the purchase price if the deal does not close. Nonrefundable earnest money is often referred to as "*hard money.*" Hard money is money you do not get back if you decide not to close on the deal. All of the deposited earnest money typically goes hard once the feasibility period ends, and therefore you lose it if you don't close.

The PSA will also typically outline a *closing period* that begins after the feasibility ends. You will also want to negotiate options to extend the closing period. Extensions to closing almost always require additional earnest money, and often this additional payment is not applicable to the purchase price. Keep in mind that you will typically want the longest feasibility period you can get while the seller will want to keep it as short as possible. The length of the feasibility period can often influence the purchase price. Sellers are often anxious to close the sale and get paid.

On the other hand, developers like you have a lot of other issues to consider and need more time. Issues like conducting all of the property inspections, legal review of project *title, survey* and *zoning,* getting tenants to sign LOI or leases, purchase and construction loan financing, equity arranged, and even teaming partners to set up. However, as mentioned above, sellers typically want to close quickly, and being able to close quickly can often result in being the winning bidder for a project. Closing quickly on the purchase of a property can often be the reason buyers get the purchase price they want. Purchasing an existing commercial real estate building can be risky business, and choosing between more time to conduct diligence or a cheaper purchase price is just one example. In any event, it is important for the developer to ask and answer all the important diligence questions during the feasibility period, including asking and answering all of the issues related to rehabbing/repairing the building and making the building suitable for the tenants and users.

Finally, there is often a long period of time between what appears to be the end of the feasibility period and the beginning of the closing period. Typically this is because you negotiate a *contingency* event. A contingency event is where closing is extended until the contingency is satisfied. In our surgery center model you could, for example, negotiate a ninety-day feasibility period with a thirty-day close. However, you may have also negotiated closing to be contingent on your obtaining financing for the purchase. Another typical contingency might be receipt from the city of permitting approval for the rehab and repair work. In any event, once a PSA is agreed to between buyer and seller, the contract is typically deposited along with the earnest money with a title company and the feasibility period begins.

THE DUE DILIGENCE AND FEASIBILITY PERIOD

Once you have entered into the earnest money contract to purchase the project, the due diligence and feasibility period begins. Remember the early diligence prior to putting the project under contract was limited; enough to understand if there were any major costs or issues that would add considerable time, expense, or risk in purchasing the building or project. Now you must go beyond the initial assessment and contract with the professionals to conduct a full diligence and determine what the real cost of the rehab and repair will be. To do this effectively, you and the hired professionals need to look once again at all aspects of the project and building(s).

There are some obvious simple things the developer should ask for and review, and there are some things the hired professionals might be better suited to "diligize."

Some of the items the developer will want to see include but are not limited to the following :

All building service and *maintenance contracts, warranties, and manuals*

Current *operating budget* and a list of planned and incurred *capital expenditures* of the last few years

Inspection reports, specifically elevator, fire systems, boilers, and others

Any notices of violations from government, municipal, or property-related authorities

Existing loan documents, if any

Property tax and utility bills (current and historical) and *common area reconciliations*

Employee listing and payroll register, if any (maintenance personnel)

All insurance policies, certificates, incidents, or *loss history* and *underwriting data*

A *personal property* inventory, such as phone, computer systems and software

Review for updates or changes to surrounding streets, highways, and access points

Site/floor and building plans

Building permits and *certificates of occupancy*

Operating management agreements

Parking issues and parking area drainage

Historical *appraisals*, engineering, and environmental reports

Signage, signage structures, plans, and restrictions

List of contractors who have worked on the building and systems

ADA (Americans with Disabilities Act) compliance

Examine and inspect the building roof and exterior/support walls and foundation, determine if the building meets applicable code including fire safety systems and handicap accessibility requirements, assess all utilities to the building and tenant usage or projected need. All major building systems, including *mechanical, electrical, and plumbing ("MEP")*, in this regard the *air conditioning systems*, or *HVAC*, boiler systems, and elevators, should be a primary focus as they can be expensive and time consuming to repair or replace. In addition, these systems and others are often tied to a computer system or outside service for operations.

For existing buildings you will need to have an *environmental phase one (asbestos, mold, lead paint)* inspection and report (you can't get a purchase or construction loan without a clean environmental report). You will want to request or find the final "*as-builts*," which are the architectural plans and specs (drawings) for how the building was completed. While you and your diligence personnel focus on building and surrounding parking and land issues, your lawyer should focus on key legal issues. These are :

Title search and policy

Survey

Property tax payments

Estoppel letters (tenant and mortgage)

Geotechnical reports and/or *seismic issues* as applicable

Zoning, licenses, occupancy certificates, and permits

Review of the *reciprocal easement agreement*, or *REA*, and/or *master declaration*. The *REA* or *master dec* is basically a set of community rules and regulations for a commercial real estate development involving more than one tenant, user, or entity to govern the project.

Litigation history

The developer will need to know that there is clean title to the property, no issues with the survey, and that the property is or can be properly zoned and licensed for the intended use. Once the developer and the professionals can adequately and thoroughly inspect the site, building, systems, and surrounding area, they can assess the work required and issue a *scope of work* and estimated cost. With the scope of work in hand, the developer can estimate the total cost and time to complete the work and therefore create a budget and schedule. The additional information provided by the scope of work will help determine the extent and cost of the rehab. In addition, you should now have the information needed to help complete the financing analysis, and of course this information may also help you renegotiate the purchase price with the seller.

If you are planning to finance the purchase simultaneously with the diligence related to the project, you must be working all the other important issues not directly related to refurbishment and repair, issues such as getting tenants to sign LOIs or lease agreements, completing negotiations, and documentation with the bank and equity financing partners.

IF THE BUILDING HAS TENANTS

Although the example we use for this section is an empty commercial building purchased to rehab, it is possible that you might find an older building in need of repair that has a tenant or two. If this is the case, you will have some additional homework during the due diligence period. You will need to review the following :

All existing leases, any addendum and riders, tenant rental increases

Common area expenses, pro rata allocation, share and allocation history, possible *caps* on specific expenses

Lease term commencement, expiration dates, and lease *options to extend*

Tenant insurance

Tenant files, which should include tenant financials, communication history, and any exclusive or new tenant or building changes approval rights

Signage or parking rights

Tenant improvement work (if not completed)

Letters of intent for new tenants

Leasing broker and any outstanding commissions or prospects

If there are existing tenants then you will also need to take a closer look at the building or project financials. This should include a close look at all financial records, including but not limited to annual profit and loss statements, balance sheet, and rent roll, as well as the current year budgets and performance, general ledger reports, CAM reconciliations, and next year's budget estimates or pro forma, tenant revenue or sales reports as applicable, and aged receivables. Of course, if there is an audit and an auditor for financial performance, this would be a great resource for diligence.

CLOSING THE PURCHASE

So let's assume you have completed the diligence and have decided to move forward and close on purchasing the building or project. The developer in closing on the purchase must now close on the financing of the project, pay the seller, contract with the engineers, architect and general contractor, secure the required permits and licenses, and begin the rehabilitation and repair construction to make the project suitable for the tenants and users. One final point: the rehab assessment conducted during feasibility is your best guess at the problems and costs! It may not reflect the actual design, engineering, structural changes, and costs that are required as the overall rehab actually occurs. This is another reason to find architects, *engineers*, and contractors experienced in the product type and tenant use. For this reason it is also wise to build a *contingency cost* into the project budget. It is likely, if not probable, that the project will incur unanticipated costs or overruns once actual construction begins.

Finally, you must turn this rehab development effort into a completed project; finishing the construction, hiring *building management*, getting the tenants moved in and paying rent, and generally *managing and operating* the now rehabbed, functioning commercial real estate project open to and serving the community.

EPILOGUE

As may be apparent from this book, the development of commercial real estate can be complicated. The developer is expected to understand all of the components and elements needed to complete a commercial real estate project, whether it is a new development or a refurbishment of an existing project. As the developer, you are the main force behind the project and responsible for leading each and every aspect of the project's success. The investors, team members, partners, local community leaders, and even tenants and users will look to you for leadership, strength, vision, knowledge, and experience related to the project.

The objective of this book and the books to follow is to attempt to break down some of the more important aspects of commercial real estate development to the fundamental component parts, therefore presenting to the reader a step-by-step guide to help in meeting or exceeding personal goals and objectives.

INDEX

OTHER BOOKS BY
ROBERT A. WEHRMEYER

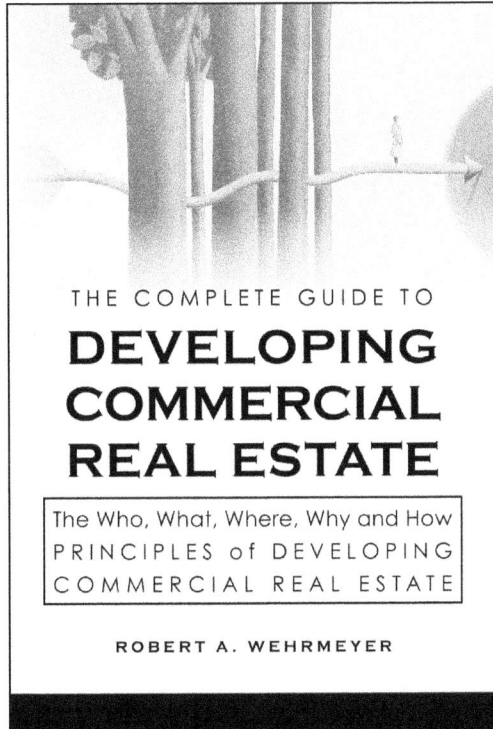

THE COMPLETE GUIDE TO
DEVELOPING
COMMERCIAL
REAL ESTATE

The Who, What, Where, Why and How
PRINCIPLES of DEVELOPING
COMMERCIAL REAL ESTATE

ROBERT A. WEHRMEYER

Purchase today at

Amazon Books and Kindle

or visit

www.wehrventures.com

www.ingramcontent.com/pod-product-compliance
Lightning Source LLC
Chambersburg PA
CBHW051352200326
41521CB00014B/2545